WISDOM TO INSPIRE

VOL.2
A BOOK OF POETRY
THE SPOKEN WORD

WISDOM TO INSPIRE

VOL.2
A BOOK OF POETRY
THE SPOKEN WORD

DESMOND S. SKYERS

To order additional copies of this book, contact:
Xlibris
800-056-3182
www.Xlibrispublishing.co.uk
Orders@Xlibrispublishing.co.uk
801730

CONTENTS

DEDICATION

This work is dedicated to my six beloved biological children Tamesha, Jahvania, Desmond Jr, Devania, Michael and Latia, and my beloved foster son Mekhi-Michael.

I also dedicate this work to my six grandchildren; my two awesome and beautiful granddaughters Khaleesi and Milah, and my five grandsons; Jomall, Jaheil, Carter, Caleb and Malekhi.

This work is also dedicated to my three beloved sisters, Lesley, Paulette and Claudine, they are in-indeed friends of Humanity and the universe.

Special dedication and love to my beloved mother, a person who lived her life caring for those who had life the hardest.

Thanks Mom.

DESMOND S. SKYERS
Jaddoka

INTRODUCTION

Wisdom to inspire is a book of poems, Collection of words designed to inspire, motivate and encourage right thoughts and right actions. These poems come from the depths of my soul, from the very essence of who I am. Poems that tells stories, simple stories of where I have been, what I have seen and heard of the nature of people, places and things. Poems, that come from experiences lived, experiences that gave me strength to live and grow into the person I am today.

It was out of sadness, fear, regrets, joy, laughter and the pain of loneliness that I wrote these poems. Psychologically and emotionally invested, writing each poem provided a psychological release for me. It was a therapeutic endeavour to the degree that after each writing I was left in a place of peace with a sense of ease.

Each poem has its own message. There is something in each one for each of us. There are poems about the rivers, the climate, the woman, the man, mental illness, spousal abuse, love, pain and even about the mirror.

I have been writing poetry for over 18 years, but it was not until a dear friend and brother in the struggle, (Brother Emmanuel Shabazz) read some of his poems to me that I began to chronicle the ones I had written and began to write new ones.

One of my earliest poems, titled **The Essence of Love**, is one of those poems that reflect a time when news that my life partner was moving on with her life had begun to sink in. It was a sad period for me, more than sadness it was a period of reflection. A state of all my "what ifs', the "could have been" "should have been" and how "I wish it were".

Two of my later poems; the first of which is titled **A letter from Ma' Daddy** and the second titled **If only I was There** are poems to my children, asking for their forgiveness. They are poems of confession, confessing the sadness of not being there, to watch as my children grow up into these beautiful young men and women they are today.

Wisdom to inspire is my way of saying thanks to the universe, thanks to humanity and thanks to the unseen powers that kept my mind, body and soul safe from harm, enabling me to survive and to live, finding self and peace in the hardest of days and the most difficult of circumstances and condition.

I pray these poems, my words and my thoughts, bring each reader a sense of joy and peace, that each reader will be inspired and motivated in their own way.

Thanks, and thanks again.

Peace

ACKNOWLEDGEMENT

It would have been impossible for me to have completed this project without the continuous help and support from the many people who took an interest in seeing the idea of **WISDOM TO INSPIRE** manifested into a book.

I will never forget the many friends and family members whose kind words and simply put, potent advice kept me going even when I wanted to give up. The sometimes critical, yet useful words, advice, and remarks from these beautiful individuals, kept me focus, dedicated and helped to make the task of writing this book one of pure joy and emotional satisfaction.

I know it would be impossible for me to include the names of all these beautiful people here, nevertheless those whose names are not included are no less important or appreciated.

A special thank from the bottom of my heart to all my friends and family members who knowingly and unknowingly encouraged, inspired and motivated me as I moved from one stage to next in the materialization of this project.

To Danny Livingston, Delroy Buckley, to Baldwin Rose, Brother Floyd Stanhope Francis, to Brother Emmanuel Shabazz, Clement Knight, Richard Kerr, Adhemar Caphaien, Kirvan Cole, Errol S. Evans, Mr. Lal Bhatia and Mr. Suresh Chand; Brothers, thank you very much, your kinds words and support are most appreciated.

To Empress Lisa Davy, Dr Cassandra Conteh and Sharon McKenzie my friends for life, many thanks to each of you for believing in me and loving me.

To my six brothers Andy, Johnny, Collin, Vincent, Audley and Marvin, words cannot express my gratitude to you all, for your ever-present support and encouragement, thank you a thousand times.

To my three awesome sisters Lesley, Paulette and Claudine, I say thanks. I know all three of you have my back. I cannot say thanks enough you guys helped me to find myself when I most needed a friend to each of you I say thanks and thanks again.

Finally, I would not be true to God and the universe, if I failed to say thanks to my beautiful and strong mother, a graceful and kind lady. Through the words of pearl from your lips I learned how to navigate my way through this wretched world, thanks Mom.

Peace

I wrote this poem at a time when I was starting to appreciate knowledge. I could barely read when I went to prison, but nine years in, I took the decision to go back to school. It was at this point I began to learn and understand the importance of education. The joy I felt from learning gave birth to this title Wisdom to Inspire.

WISDOM TO INSPIRE

She is a fountain spring forth; fresh, crystal clear,
Transparent, a sparkling gem.

A sound, even a squeak,
From her lips, the universe speak.

The atmosphere, stratosphere,
Watch and listen, she is always there.
Her words are in the air,
In her eyes a distance stare.

Her eyes are like stars in the night sky,
To guide you to the nearest rest, no need to question why?
She is there to wipe tears from your eyes.

Tears of joy, tears of pain,
Then it rains, showers of rain.

Soaring like an eagle, dropping from above,
Sitting on the windowsill, humble as a dove.

Wisdom between her lips, a sword,
The paths she travels, the ancient road
Not a cat, rat nor a toad

Shock, black and exact,
Like a mountain to climb, she is a standing rock.

So be still now and listen,
Have a case to make, just give the reason.
She is here with us for all seasons

Wisdom! Oh wisdom!
Wisdom to inspire!

A word, a smile or even a simple thought,
A wink, a nod, sounds to make you laugh,
From her words, you are sure to get a blast!

Food for the flesh, food for the soul, food of wisdom,
For she is a fountain spring forth, crystal clear, a sparkling gem
At her side, we to pray to be again.

In her bosom, we dream to lay,
For her love, we wish to die.
A laugh, a hiss, a sigh.
Sounds to make us cry.

For its wisdom!
Wisdom to inspire!

A fountain,
A sparkling gem.

Oh wisdom! Wisdom to inspire!

19/1/2013

I am my mother's son, growing up with a single mother I learned and saw the strength, care, and intelligence of the woman. I came to understand her pain and her struggles. This poem is in honour of all women, out there who see in their children potential that their children fail to see in themselves. This was the case with me, my mother saw in me, that which I did not see in myself.

THE WOMAN THE WOMAN, THE WOMAN

Mother, Aunty, Sister, Daughter, Wife,

Once a little girl,
A precious gift to the world,
A lady,
Nine months carrying the baby.

Our first nourisher makes us stronger,
She is our first teacher, makes us wiser,
A perfect guide, a care giver

She is the womb of creation, triple darkness,
Deserving nothing but the best!
A **Princess**,
Queen, an **Empress,**
Respect!

Why calling her out of her name?
Causing her heartache and pain?
Other than her name,
Plan to defame.

You must be crazy!
A woman of integrity,
Moving with such grace, and tranquillity,
Don't you know, she is the soul of humanity?

With your hands, on her you love to hit,
On her confidence, you dare to pick.
A part of it,
Saying it's her loving that you miss.
Her intelligence you try to "diss."

Not knowing she is your equal,
Treat her well so you can reach your full potential,
180 degrees universal; she is special.

She was here from the beginning,
Giving true meaning
To the plants, trees and everything living.

In all creation
Treat her as number one.

So, beautiful she is,
What will become of you and me?
If we fail to let her be
Like a tree,
Planted by a river of water bringing life to you and me.

She brought us into this world.
Teaching us from her lips words of pearl,
Stories to carry us through this wretched world.

For her we live, and so be it,
If we must, for her we will surely die.
Without her, there is nothing in this world for you nor me.

The woman! The woman! The woman!

17/2/07

I was at place in my life where the desire to do the right thing had become more powerful than the desire for instant gratification. I wanted to do the right thing and be seen and known as one doing what was right. However as I began to make my moves to the right path I began to see and experience the irony of contradiction. Morality, whose morality?

MORALITY, MORALITY, WHO'S MORALITY?

Make sure to take heed,
That you do not plant seed
To create animosity and hatred,
Bringing chaos and war where people live at ease.

Nothing wrong with a little thank you, and a yes please,
Its words like these
That brings peace and calm, even in the rough seas.

Living in a world of diversity,
Where there is respect for one's religion, race and ethnicity,
The building blocks of society.

An extended hand is a necessity.
Visiting the prisoners, caring for the
sick and feeding the hungry,
Still it might just be,
What is good for you, is bad for me.

Nevertheless, whatever we do, we do with integrity,
Our words and actions will determine the depth of our sincerity.

For the virtue of life are the lights society,
Remembering our duty to humanity;
Bringing forward fruits of stability;
Creating a climate of unity;
Peace, justice and equality.

Do unto others, as you would want done to you,
An old saying, designed, as a guide for me and you.
And even the power few

Morality, Oh yes! Morality.
Is the wisdom of conscience
In our desires to exercise patience,
Wise words to the ignorant, even to the wise and prudent.

Morality, morality, whose morality?

04/22/2008

As I reflect, looking back, way back; back to when I was just a baby, well as far back as I could remember and as far as I could see and understand there was only one constant in my life and that was my mother. My beautiful mother, who gave her all, for the care of her children. A beautiful black queen, who have instilled her soul into her children.

As I reflect, it is clear to me, every day is Mother's Day, because it was every day that she was my mother, and even now as she has journey to her place of rest, she is still with me, her soul she poured in me, and so for her and all the mothers out there I wrote this poem titled Every day is mother's day

EVERY DAY IS MOTHER'S DAY

So, they set aside a day,
And called it Mother's Day.
Well, for me every day is Mother's Day.

Remember when you were a little child
and your mommy went away?
How you would cry, asking why mommy went away?
And when she came back you acted
as if you didn't want to play?
Well, every day is Mother's Day

I got love for my daddy,
But thank God for my mommy.

Stories of old,
Stories that she told.
A guidance from the depth of her soul,
A warning so precious, a warning so bold!

My first teacher,
Words from her lips makes me wiser.
A lesson she taught that made me stronger.
From her hands, a touch so tender,
Guidance that makes me think a little harder.

Got love for my daddy
But thank God for my mommy

A woman so beautiful, a woman so strong!
Do unto others, a lesson she taught me how to understand.
And even though she always held my tiny little hand,
She never let me get away with doing
something that was wrong.

Remember when mommy got you your first toy?
A doll for a girl, a truck for a boy?
And when you felt sad, she wouldn't let you cry?
And then she baked a cake, a pumpkin pie?
A beautiful mother brings tears to your eyes,

A got love for my daddy,
But thank God for my mommy!

Nine months she carried me,
From a baby, up through elementary,
At her side, how I loved to be.

Words from her lips made me ponder,
Bedtime stories that made me wonder,
True love, it's hard to find another.

And when I had the flu,
Sleepless night she went through.

A mommy is always there,
For her child, her love she willingly share,
Just for you, to show she really cares.

A loyal friend,
The truth she never bends.
Like an angel sent,
A helping hand, she always lend.

Set aside a day,
And called it Mother's Day,
Well, for me every day is Mother's Day.

A faithful friend, one of a kind,
Traveling distance, through space and time
A mother and her child forever bind.

Blessed love, blessed love,
A word of peace to all the Mothers there,
Beautiful souls, ooh! So dear.

5/9/2013

The consequences came home in the form of solitary confinement, those days the only thoughts were simple ones, like a glimpse of the dawning Sun and so I wrote this poem. Writing this poem provided an essence of freedom for me, I saw the life that I once knew and could at the time of writing this poem only dream of.

THE DAWNING SUN

How I wish to see a dawning sun,
A dawning sun.
The days are long, the days are lonely;
How I wish for a moment, a minute in the dawning sun.

So, bright a light that glows,
Warmth flows
A distance row,
Betwixt two patches of cloud, a rainbow,
In the wake of the morning, a time to plant, a time to sow.

Then woe! Woe is me,
How I wish to see, how I wish to see.

Whether under a tree or a shade out yonder,
Then, it won't matter,
For I would have walk the path where the ancients wonder.

To a place above a tree, upon a hill, a hill so high
It touches the sky.

How I hope to get a glimpse, a glimpse of a dawning sun,
Who knows? Tomorrow the rains might come.

Doors closed, windows locked,
Drapes drawn; darkness wrapped.
Chilly days, cold nights,
Not a ray in sight.

How I wish to see,
How I wish to see.

But it's raining now, though outside I cannot see,
I can hear the showers; showers of water falling from the sky.

The days are long, the days are lonely,
Just a moment away, and just maybe,
For minute I would get to see,

A dawning sun,
A dawning sun

02/09/2013

All I had was time, time behind walls and razor wire fence; lock doors where rule and regulations were maintained with a steel hand. With time on my hands, I spend a lot of time watching CNN, watching the news was hard at times, On a constant basis, the news would have some form of report on the killing of an unarmed black inner city youth by members of law enforcement and police.

For most of us locked behind the walls and razor wire fence we cried for our children, we worried about our sons, and we prayed for them, we saw these killing from the point of view of the victims and these victims were family.

MAKES ME ANGRY

Makes your blood boil!
Makes you recoil!
Another black child being racially profiled!

It wasn't anything that he did, it wasn't anything that he do,
They didn't have to shoot you,
Hands in plain sight, hands in plain view,
They didn't have to shoot you!

Its regression, oppression
Yes discrimination!

Makes me angry!
Really, really, angry!

Ask a mother or a father in the black community,
Up against the wall, an everyday reality,
When they see a cop, they say, they see the enemy.

They may shout, scream and raise their voices!
But mommy to her son, you must play nice,
Freedom of speech, but you have no other choice.

Stop and frisk, stop and frisk,
Don't touch your wallet,
Gun shots! And they rarely ever miss.

Every day, new laws on the books,
Laws to criminalized, turning children into crooks.
Can't find your son, in a jail cell you must look.

Lock them up, lock them up!, and throw away the key,
A million black men in the penitentiary,
Never have a date, nor a day to be free!

Could it be?
A war against the black family?
No! They say, but they could have fooled me.

Makes me angry!
Really, angry!

When they see a Cop, they say, they see the Enemy,
Ask a mother and Father in the black community.

No matter how kind, no matter how humble,
Putting food on the table,
Life and death for some people.

A word of peace to all the family,
Who lost a son or a daughter to youth violence?
Or at the hands of the police.

06/06/2013

They mean the world to me, and I wanted to say I am sorry. I am so sorry. sorry for not being there for them, four beautiful daughters growing without their father. At times, when I would think of them, tears would just roll down the sides of my face. It felt like each drop of tear had its own story, its own pain.

How could I let them know I was thinking of them, what could I say, they were babies when I went away. Years away, not knowing how or what to say.

IF ONLY I WAS THERE a beautiful poem to my four daughters and young girls growing up without their dad.

IF ONLY I WAS THERE

So much time, so much time,

Years have passed
Since I saw you last,
In a trap, your dad got caught.

Years away on a wondering path,
Locked in my heart,
A tiny baby girl, having a funny little laugh

A precious moment with her, from the start,
Now it seems, time have moved so fast.
So much time, so much time,
So much time have passed, since I saw you last.

My beloved daughter, if only I was there,
Then you would have known you have dad who really cares,

One to take you to a park or to take you to a fair,
Just to lend a helping hand, to get up the stairs.

A beloved daughter, a child so dear,
To share a laugh, a cry or to wipe away a tear,
A moment of doubt or a moment of fear

Day and night, it's her eyes that I see,
There I was face to face with reality.
Moments like those I wished I was free,
Then I could see,
As she made and created history

So much time, so much time, so much time has passed,
Since I saw you last

How I wish, I was there to teach her about this wretched world,
Dropping knowledge more precious than diamonds or pearls,
Spending precious time with my little girl

Out on the town, a son with his mommy,
A daughter with her daddy,
Fun time at the movie,
Or even a trip down to Disney,
Making memories for eternity

I heard your mommy sent you off to college,
Sorry I wasn't there to fix you up a little package,
And leave you a note with a simple little message.

A special young lady, high above the average,
Life without your daddy could have cost
a lifetime worth of damage,
But thank God, your mommy found a way to manage.

So much time, so much time,
The future is yours; the past is mine,
A prayer for your forgiveness, an act so kind,
But if you never find the time

It's okay, it's okay,
Just a little baby when I first went away.

I do understand,
In another life, I am sure to correct this wrong,
Then I hope to be a dad, worthy of
giving away a daughter's hand.

Some may ask, "Why mention this?"
But it's the simple things in life with you I miss."
A hug, a laugh, a simple kiss,
Moments like those, with you are price-less.

So much time, so much time,
So much time has passed
Since I saw you last.

8/28/2013

This poem was written in honour to black history month, just my way of joining my voice to the struggle of a people that brought me into this world, such an honour to be called by their names. GREETINGS AND PEACE; and so the celebration of recognition Black Africans contribution to the western world has begun.

GREETINGS AND PEACE, GREETINGS AND PEACE

Just another black brother in the belly of the beast
Greetings and peace,
Greetings and peace

Another black brother in the belly of the beast
The Gods are watching,
Grown me cartooning

Mind-set; mind-set on the frenzy
Black brothers fighting for a place in society,
A task made hard, by white supremacy.

Then they say any means necessary,
The X property
The ends justify the means, Machiavelli.

Up against the powers that be,
A path to find your own identity

Cries of pain, pain I feel none.
Like father, like son.
Wealth from the father to the son,
But we had none.

Greetings and peace,
Greetings and peace
Just another black brother in the belly of the beast

Thoughts traveling 24 billion miles per second,
Secret societies, twilight zones, how long will this shit last?
A life without a past,
Knowledge of self, self-lost.

Rockefeller, the Illuminates,
Serving up food laced with Prozac.
Some sitting in the dope gap
Now with a little push back,
Young brothers and sisters building
consciousness block by block

Getter stronger,
Knowledge coming from the east to the west
Training and practice to be the best,
To meet and overcome every test

Greetings and peace,
Greetings and peace,
Another black brother in the belly of the beast

How could it be?
Mother Africa and what do you see?

Natural wealth,
Physical wealth,
Spiritual wealth

Yet animosity and hatred,
Strong brothers wasted.

Brothers killing brothers,
What's up with my soul brother?
Roots brother,
Blood brother

Brothers looking out their windows,
From a project high in the sky,
Sky high

Brains fry,
Looking around wishing to die

But mummy will cry,
Leaving the children with tears in their eyes

Love, peace and justice or is it just-us

Greeting and peace,
Greetings peace,
Just another black brother in the belly of the beast

Greeting and peace,
Greeting and peace,
Just another black brother in the belly of the beast

08/05/2013

This poem is one of my later ones, as a member of the Rastafarian teaching I held the belief that a king was to come and that the king did came so in 2013 I wrote this poem in honour of the King and in celebration of the Rastafarian celebration of his coronation.

IT WAS WRITTEN, A KING WAS TO COME

It was written.
A king was to come,
A King was to come.

1930, 2nd November,
The day was at hand,
For His Imperial Majesty's Coronation

From near and far, from every nation,
People came in the tens and in the thousands.
All bearing witness, to the crowning of a black man

To the leaders of the world, the truth was known
Look to the East, Prince is found.
A black Prince, to sit upon the ancient throne,
Upon his head to wear the Golden Crown.

Yes, a King was to come,
A King was to come.

The King was to come, and the King did came,
To rule over a people, called by his name
Having one goal, having one aim

Ruling for neither wealth nor fame,
But whether through joy, or whether through pain,
A sacrifice to the people; the King had nothing to gain.

The lands to the East, straight out of Africa,
A new name was heard, first echoed from Jamaica.
A beautiful island, of wood and water,
Then from the mouth of its people; you heard the chant,

Rasta!
Rasta!

Long live the King of Ethiopia
Kings of Kings, Lords of Lords, the conquering
lion of the tribe of Judah.
Reggae music and a new culture,
Pick up the chalice, load up the ganja.

Ital stew, with sweet potato,
Bobo Shanty, Nihya Binghi and the 12 tribes order,
Rasta! Rasta!

For a king was to come,
A King was to come.

At first the news was heard just by a few,
Conscious brothers did what they had to do.
Much tribulation they had to go through,
Raising the red, gold and green; replacing
the red white and blue

Honour to the King,
Honour to the King

For a King was to come,
A King was to come.

Let your dreadlocks fly,
Raise the red, gold and green banner high!
Then chant the new song,

Tafari!
Tafari!

His Imperial Majesty,
Emperor Haile Selassie I,
Ever living, ever faithful Jah! Rasta far I

11/02/1997

I began to study black history in the late 1990s, growing up amongst the Rastafarians, the history and struggle of black people was front and centre in our culture.

Understanding of this history, this struggle, I decided to write this poem, trying to tell the story through poetry. At times, I was deep in my feelings, I was at a place in my journey, where I saw the plight of young inner-city youths as one tied to the history of slavery and the Jim Crow south.

This was my way of giving voice to the plight and sojourn of my fore-parents, 400 years has passed, and it seems the condition in one form or another in regards to the conditions of black people living in the west and all over the world remains the same.

So in honour of Black history month, recognizing Black Africans contribution in the development of the new world and as a reminder of the pain of racism and the continued struggles of Black people on the shores of the Americas, I wrote this poem.

400 YEARS, 400 YEARS

Two hundred and forty-four years of slave labour,
One hundred years of segregation and murder,
Ku Klux Klan from Texas to Alabama,
Tennessee to Georgia

400 years, 400 years

Encoded in the DNA of America,
The blood sweat and tears of Black Africa.
Buffalo soldier, fighting for America

Poncho Villa
Across the border
Underground Railroad up into Canada
Black African contribution forever,
However

Today, over the airwaves, you can hear racial epithets,
Out on the streets, black youths becoming white targets
A son out to the store, a black mother must fret,
So far, are we free yet?

40 acres and a Mule, a promise never kept
Reparation a goal we set

Could be your son,
My son,
How far have we come?
When an innocent youth, must run,
From the nozzle of a gun

400 years, 400 years

Stand your ground,
Stand your ground,
Then a gunshot sound!
Another black youth shot down.

Straight through his heart,
Another young life lost,
A life that barely got start

A jury of peers, or a jury of friends,
To all black youths the message was sent,
Come around the bend,
And your young life could surely end.

Lower your gaze,
If you want to live out half your days,
A black president, but no one cares,
Racism and racial profiling continues unfazed.

400 years, 400 years

01/26/2013

I wrote this poem 2014, this was the year when my beloved mother went off to her resting place, I had the opportunity to watch the service and the celebration from my prison cell, yes it was a celebration. I will never forget the sadness I felt, yet I was overwhelmed with joy as I watched how people had travelled from near and far, coming to say their goodbyes to my beloved mother.

I grew up at my mother's side, seeing how she would give her last even to a stranger, she meant the world to me yes, she did everything for me, such a beautiful soul. And there she was on her way and I was not there to say goodbye.

This poem helps me to not only express my love for her and to reflect but more importantly, this is a poem that helps me to come to reality with her passing.

Sorry mom that I was there say goodbye, you represent the best of God's creation. A MOTHER'S LOVE!

A MOTHER'S LOVE

A mother's love,
A mother's love

Always there for me,
There for me,
Even when she never ate, she had food for me.
Day and night, she worked for me
She bought clothes for me,
And where I rest my head, she paid the rent for me.

Taught me well and let me be,
She did her best for me,

A mother's love,
A mother's love

Never wanted to see me in a fight,
Little Desi got mad, but Mummy was right,
Tippy toes in the middle of the night,
To give her baby boy a kiss good night

Bedtime stories, to make me fall asleep
She have love for me, a love so deep,
When she had to get the belt, little Desi had to feel the heat,
Bad little kid had to get him off the street.

A thousand years may pass,
Still to her it's neither a duty nor a task,
It's her love, a care that will forever last.

A mother's love,
A mother's love

Words are not enough to say how much you are appreciated.
Nine children, a blessing that you were created
Early in the morning and off she goes
Never to the movie or a show
But its workflow

A mother's love,
A mother's love

A special thanks to you Mum

05/12/2014

I wrote this poem during a period when I had begun to come to grips with the facts of doing time in a privately-run institution where things were materially different from doing time in a government operated institution

Had to find strength, this was nine months after prisoners' riot, setting the institution on fire. Conditions at this private institution was atrocious to say the least, prisoners were treated like animals or worst.

During the riot, a guard was killed, and for this we were punished beyond belief and so I wrote this poem, trying to find reason to hope, reason to live.

THE WEIGHT OF A STRAW

The loads of today are but the weight of a straw,
For the responsibilities of tomorrow are ones for the ages,

And ones for the ink of the historians
It's not about who right or who is wrong
Its information
For future generation

Bear well today then
And be glad it's only your back that is bent
And not your knees as well

Pain is the price we must pay for the life we choose,
Respect they say is due, to who respect is due,

Depending who
And what you do
At times, respect will only go to a few.

So bear well,
Bear well,

For the loads of today are but the weight of a straw

10/31/2013

This was the first time in my life that I felt alone, and I was alone.

CAN'T STOP, WON'T STOP

Can't stop, won't stop now you look back

Then she was my baby,
Then she was my lady.

Then she was my girl,
Diamonds and pearl,
Trips around the world.

Bora Bora, Acapulco,
Espresso, cappuccino,
Breakfast up in the Pocono.

Cash flow,
Prada, Gucci, Polo,
Never thought my baby would have let me go,
But she did, yes, she did on the Southside of Chicago.

Can't stop,
Won't stop now you look back.

Can't stop, won't stop
Now you look back.

Living on the edge,
Never let money go to your head,
For a dollar, Honey never had to beg.

A go getter, got to get mine,
Tickets to the game, got seats on the sideline,
Left her a note, dropped her a line.

A smile on her face was a telling little sign
38-26-42, Honey so fine.

VIP section
Flashes of fashion
Trips to the motherland

Pushing 140,
Black Lamborghini,
Sipping on rose.

In a blink of an eye, lighting flashed,
Then everything crashed!
Hands above my head, hands behind my back,
Everyone thought
Honey got my back.

Can't stop,
Won't stop,
Now you look back.

Then she was my baby,
Then she was my lady.

Then she was my girl,

Diamonds and pearl,
Trips around the world.

Had to move on
A new day had dawn
Left outside, standing on the lawn

Can't stop,
Won't stop,
Now you look back.

Then she was my baby,
Then she was my lady.

Then she was my girl

Diamonds and pearl,
Trips around the world.

Then she was my girl

11/19/1998

I didn't know I could write, after all when I arrived into the prison system, I could barely read. The idea that I would become a writer was the last thing on my mind, even more, nowhere in my thinking did I see poetry.

This poem was one written to a special person and for a special person, I will not reveal her name here, I am hopeful that one day I will get to tell her how much she meant to me, that she was my PURPLE PURPOSE ROSE, the inspiration for this poem.

A PURPLE PURPOSE ROSE

I rose to the sight and scent of a purple purpose rose,
A purple purpose rose, staring through my window.

Beauty veil, fingers and toes I could not see,
Beyond her face I did not see.
Height and shape, I wondered, an angel, could it be?

The beauty of sapphire,
Radiant in dark matter,
Melanin proper.

A glimpse of teeth, teeth so white,
Snow white, pearl white,
A beautiful morning sight.

A purple purpose rose,
A purple purpose rose, peering through my window.

Through her eyes, her soul revealed
In her heart, her wisdom sealed
A mind to mend, a soul to heal.

Then I said,
"This must be a blessing,
A blessing, from above".

How I wish, with her to be,
To my heart, she has found the key,
A trip around the world, across the deepest sea.

It's a rose, the scent of a purple purpose rose;
A pearl, a sapphire,
A purple purpose rose staring through my window.

02/07/2013

This poem was written in honour of black history month, and a tribute to those who give their all in the struggle for equal, right and justice for an enslaved and oppressed people.

This was not supposed to be a poem, I was asked to give a speech on black history but the time that was allotted was not enough for me to say all that I wanted to say, so I decided to just write a poem.

IS IT TRUE, IS IT TRUE?

Black history, black history, who wrote the story?
Black history, black history, who wrote the story?

From elementary up through university,
A story they tell about Abraham Lincoln and slavery.

To find the truth, let's take a few steps back.

On a hunch,
Students rushing the libraries in bunch,
Skipping breakfast and even lunch.

So, they say, black history began with the Atlantic slave trade,
When names like coloured and nigger were made,
When the black family worked without being paid.

Is it true? Is it true?

In all your wars, war vet,
Black blood, black sweat,
Freedom is in the mind, mind-set,

Shackles around your feet,
Shackles around your neck,
Are we free yet?

Black history, Black history, who wrote the story?
Black history, Black history, who wrote the story?

Timbuktu, they say was the world first university,
West Africa, the empire of Ghana, Songhay and Mali,
Where wise men took council and raised their family.

Creating a state of peace and security,
Building kingdoms and civilizing humanity,

Is it true? Is it true?

That the first upright man walked up out of Africa,
The lands of the East, on the banks of river Kwanza,
Up through Asia,
Across Siberia, down into Alaska,
North and South America

Is it true? Is it true?

Flipping through the books,
A long time it took,
Africa was the seats of learning, long
before Alexander the crook.
It was written, Africans created fire and
taught the world how to cook,

Black history, Black history, who wrote the story?
Black history, Black history, who wrote the story?

Is it true? Is it true?

The history of blackness,
African likeness,
Brothers and sisters living in the West,
Racial wilderness.

In this, white rulers invest,
Teaching their brightest and their best,

The philosophy
Of Black inferiority,
And white supremacy,
Taking African children, as European property.

Black history, Black history, who wrote the story?
Black history, Black history, who wrote the story?

Brother and sisters of Kenya, made a run for the hills,
Working hard to build up their skills.
Then with courage and sheer will,
They attacked the enemies until
The battlefield stood still.

Then Kenya independence was won,
The world saw a new nation
Still, a thing we the people find hard to understand
How the powers that be has yet to say they were wrong.

Black history, Black history who wrote the story?
Black history, Black history who wrote the story?
Is it true? Is it true?

02/14/2008

I wrote this poem to say let's kiss and make up, it's for all the brothers out there who did something they have no business doing, that cause their beloved queen, empress loyal partner stress. Nothing less than a diamond, a sincere apology then reparation.

IT'S A DIAMOND

It's a diamond, a diamond, just for you,
A diamond, a diamond, just for you.

When I close my eyes and look within.
In my heart, for you, a door is open.
In a text, a letter, on paper I put my pen,
To you, these words I send.

Whatever I did, I never meant to do,
I never meant to hurt you.

Oh my!
I never want to see you cry,

In life or death,
I promised, I would never make your eyes wet.
It's my life's quest,
In you I have found a queen, my empress.

It's you, your smile inspires me,
What we share was meant to be.
A love so deep, the deep blue sea,
Making our dreams come to reality.

So it's a diamond, a diamond, just for you,
Baby it's a diamond, a diamond, just for you.

For you, nothing but the best,
The finest.
From my pay-check
To the side I set,
Cut and polished, on my life I bet.

A gem, a precious stone,
With you I hope to make my home.
A beautiful queen to sit upon the throne.

Then I closed my eyes and look within,
And in my heart, for you a door is open,
In a text, a letter, on paper I put my pen,
To you these words I send.

Whatever I did, I never meant to do
I never meant to hurt you.

Oh my,
I never want to see you cry,

For In life or death,
I promise, I would never make your eyes wet.

It's my life's quest,
In you I have found a queen, my empress.

I remember, how could I forget?
I never meant for you to leave.

What was said, was said,
You know I am not too proud to beg,

But I thought you understood,
That for you to the moon I would,

And you know I would.

So, baby, it's a diamond, a diamond, just for you,
It's a diamond, a diamond, just for you,

My beautiful queen.
A diamond just for you

02/04/1996

This poem is one of those poems that comes from a deep place within my psyche, in this poem I am saying don't give up. Find faith and keep it close to your heart.

MY NAME IS FAITH

It was a few days in my journey,
When I connected with this unusual energy,
One seems to have come from eternity.

Upon her face I could not look,
For all my strength, it have took.
What's your name, what's your name?
The earth may shake, the earth may have shook.

Fear was upon me,
For her face I could not see,
Then I heard a voice, "It's me, it's me".
Take my hand,
And let me guide you across the land".

"It's me you have hoped for, the evidence you have yet to see,
My name is Faith, take hold of me.
Wrap your arms around me,
Let me lead you to peace and prosperity".

At first, I did not understand,
Was this coming from a mortal man?
Trust and believe, there is a place in me for everyone.

Never have I heard of you now, what am I supposed to do?

"Raise your head up high,
Dry the tears from your eye,
Living in peace, as each day passes by".

"Doubtful at times?
Just remember, in me all things are fine".

"My name is Faith, my name is Faith,
Grab a hold of me,
And I will show you all there is to see".

06/08/1999

I thought it would be criminal to write a book of poetry and do not include at least one that embrace my Jamaican culture. I grew up in the street where "Nah change" was a mantra. Nah change in the streets meant to keep it real, stay true to the game and your principles.

NAH CHANGE, NAH CHANGE

Want to go home a mi yaad,
Nuh matter how tings ruff, tings caan be so haad
A game a domino an a game a caahd

Nah change! Nah change!

Nuh matta how long man live over broad
Di luv to mi people dem, dung a yaad,
Nah change! Nah change!

Long fi eat sum ackee and salt fish,
From ancient time a wi national dish.

Sum bwile dumpling and bwile banana,
A glass a rum punch, wid mi dinna,
Food fi tek mi back to mi roots and mi cultha.

Waa fi go ome a mi yaad,
Nuh matta how tings ruff, tings caan so haad.
A game a domino and a game a caahd
Nah change! Nah change!

Gimmi mi roots and mi cultha,
From a likkle pickney, wi a bun the ganja,
Nah go eat the poke, a chicken wi prehfa.

Up eena the hills or roun the caana,
Tek a stroll dung a de beach wid mi likkle dawta,
Fi go tek a likkle dip eena the sea wata.

Wudda luv a plate, a rice and peas and steam fish,
Food like dis
Cudda be de national dish,
Nah bother staat cry, a jus wish, mi a wish.

Nah change! Nah change!

Caa wait fi lisen to sum reggae music,
Haatbeat riddim, fi heal all de sick.
Rack to the beat, on yuh feet yu av fi steady an quick.

Tek har back a yaad, mek she ride de riddim,
Nickle an dime, poun and shillin,
Reggae music, fi gih yuh deep feelin.

Nah change! Nah change!

The rivas an de beach,
It nuh tek, nuh lang time fi reach.
A patois wi chat, but a English wi teach.
A Rasta wi live but a Christianity wi preach,
Land easy fi get, a piece a land you cah lease,
Summa all year roun, out a door you cah sleep.

Thunder a roll and lighting a flash,
Tek a look outside, a Usain Bolt dey pon the track.
A di faasses man, a him have the reckhaad fi dat.
Faassa dan a lion or a mounten cat.

Nah change! nah change!

Wa go home a mi yaad,
Tings cah be so ruff, things cah be so haad.

02/02/1998

This poem was written to reflect a certain degree of social consciousness, issues relating to pollution, the polluting of our rivers, seas, oceans and other sources of water are dear to my heart. I grew up around water, the river that run through my hometown, was a place of refuge for us growing up.

We love our rivers and springs, they represent the soul of our community, today as we travels to the banks of our rivers our heart pained. Whether it's plastic bags, containers or other sources of pollutants, it's clear to me that we could be doing permanent damage to our rivers and sources of clean water.

RIVER, OH! RIVER

River, Oh River! Whence cometh thou?
I can hear the rippling sound as too and fro you go,
Sometimes swift, sometime slow.

There you go,
There you go.
Sound so clear as you ebb and flow.

On your banks I sometimes sit and at
your majestic power I stare,
Staring out into a water, so powerful and crystal clear.
A place to go, my soul to bear.

On your banks I sit and listen.
Listening, as the elders' reason,
To a person,
From you we have learned so many lessons.

River, Oh, River!

As far as my eyes can see,
Calm and quiet you sometimes be,
Snaking your way down through the valley,
Out to the mouth of the sea
Dumping your black mud for all the eyes see.

Down your banks where the waters meet,
You nourish the soil for the plants we eat.

River, Oh River!

On your banks great cities are made
From your thick mud impurities fade
Yet today, islands of plastic, an eco-system to be save

From the Nile to the Mississippi
River Kwanza and the Rio Grande
So much good you have done for humanity
Water for the poor, water for the needy

River, Oh, River!
On your banks I take my seat,
You're rippling sound, my stress relief,
Signs of pollution and for you the people weep.

Out in the deep the children swim and splash,
Even though, on you the world has turned its back.

As far as the eyes can see,
The water buffalo, the warthog even a donkey,
Animals of every variety.

On your banks prey and predator alike
Sometime in peace, then again for food they often fight,

From a Lion, a deer tries to flee,
Hiding amongst the plants and trees.
On your banks, oh river, a colony of wasp; a colony of bee

River, Oh River!

Cold in the winter.
But warm in the summer.

River, Oh River!

05/26/2007

The pen was inspired by a rule in the system that do not allow prisoners on transfer unit, solitary lock down or prisoners in the intake unit to have full-size pens.

In these environments, prisoners are issue a small flexible finger-size plastic pen. As a writer this poses a constant challenge, for one. Ink run out fast and it was difficult to get a new supply.

THE PEN

The pen, the pen,
Write with me, write with me,
Said the pen.

I am closer to you then a friend,
Not an ear to hear, a mouth to speak,
Have a story to tell ask the pen.

Between your fingers I love to be,
A simple word or a letter,
Write with me for the world to see.

Black, blue, red, even pink,
I am the colour of your ink.
Putting your thoughts together as you think,
Then one, by one, each word you link.

A table, a chair and a notebook,
Story to tell, get a hook.

Felt tip, ballpoint,
With me you write your first line.

Write with me,
Write with me
Said the pen.

I am closer to you then a friend.

02/04/2013

A dream in a poem, what would it be like if the idea of a God was one built on the passion, care and strength of a woman rather than the egotistic, revengeful and the so-call decisiveness nature of man?

This poem was inspired by the strength, steadfastness, dedication, discipline and determination of my beloved mother and of all the single mothers out there who in the hardest and most difficult of times, never give up, who even between her tears of wants and needs, walked that extra mile just to make sure her children have food clothes and shelter.

WHEN THE GOD WHERE WOMEN a poem of love, appreciation and gratitude to the woman.

WHEN THE GODS WERE WOMEN

When the Gods were women,
When the Gods were women.

Well then, not a dime was spent on building bombs,
There were no need for Nuclear weapon,
Words of peace and compassion,
These were tools in our hands.

Politics was to everyone,
A means to an end, where
Race was not a barrier,
Neither faith, age nor gender.
It was like a utopia

When the Gods were women,
When the Gods were women,

Kindergarten, to the university,
Science, maths, engineering and technology,
From a young age, students' mastery.

Children were schooled in safe environment,
Little boys grew up to be responsible men,
And little girls grew into wise and respectful women.

Dad would bless the dinner table,
Children would eat their vegetable,
To each other, everyone humble,
Conversations were civil.

When the Gods were women,
When the Gods were women,

The air was clean,
No global warming,
Mummy could go for a walk in the morning,
Taking her children to the park leaving her doors open.

Rain for the heaven were like pearl,
The sun brought heat that warmed our world.

Down to the seacoast,
Out in the desert,
Rain forest or the mountain peak.

Our hearts were made glad,
Not a tear for our children to have.

No need to cheat,
All our needs were meet
Front seat, back seat,
Just take a seat.

Families were made happy,
Living in peace, love and prosperity.

When the Gods were women,
When the gods were women.

01/03/2013

It took a lot to bring change to my life, the type of change that would one day turn a life of crime into a life lived at peace with oneself, of positive influence and positive motivation.

For a very long time I was drawn to negativity, a culture in which instant gratification and cynicism formed the basis for how I made my decisions, this approach led me to a life of crime and illegality. To find change I had to be born again, I had to find new company where knowledge, logics and the love of learning was front and centre in my everyday activities.

BORN GOD FROM AMONG THE GODS

When the students are ready, they will find the teacher
A light at the end of the tunnel, preparing for the future.

A teaching I have found,
That held my feet on solid ground,
Giving me ear to hear, a brand-new sound,
Words to lift me up, never to put me down.

A teaching that took me on a unique journey,
One to build a new mind, soul and body,
Enabling me to create and write a new story.

Born God, from among the Gods.

When the students are ready, they will find a teacher,
A light at the end of the tunnel, preparing for a future.

A new comfort zone and familiarity.
A new language, void of negativity or profanity,
A new mind to understand pain, struggle and adversity.

A teaching of self, God and the family,
About nations, race, kind and the community,
The universe and all that the eyes can see.

Born God, from among the Gods.

A teaching that taught me the proper use of space and time,
Sitting around all day, and you are sure to be left behind,
What you have forfeit, someone else is sure to find.

Closing the gap between thoughts and action,
Understanding the difference between right and wrong,
Hard at work, securing a new creation.

In this teaching I have grown and matured
Now I am sure,
Once a life of waste, now such a life no more,
A master teacher has given me the keys to a new door.

When the student is ready, he will find the teacher,
Like a son to a father,
360 degrees, in the cipher
To every people, there comes a messenger.

Bringing a message to a people,
Teaching by example,
Making things easy and simple,
A sample.

Born God, from among the Gods.

When the students are ready, they will find a teacher,
A light at the end of the tunnel, preparing for a future,

Born God, from among the Gods.

When the students are ready, they will find a teacher,
A light at the end of the tunnel, preparing for a future.

07/23/1999

In this poem rain is symbolic of a continuous struggle, in my journey pain and suffering was a daily reality. This poem brought a therapeutic relieve, even today when I hear the falling of rain it brings a calming effect to me.

RAIN, RAIN, RAIN

Everywhere you turn, you will hear the same refrain,
Rain, rain, rain,
Heavy rain.

Everywhere you turn, you will hear the same refrain,
Rain, rain, rain
Heavy rain.

I do not know, I cannot tell,
If its the weather or something else,
But outside, it sure looks like hell.

A day of hanging clouds, clouds so dense,
It makes no sense.

Hence, I wonder,
Would lightning and thunder,
Bring a day full of rain and rising water?

Up the block you hear the church bell,
As a preacher to the people yell,
"Get all you need today because tomorrow
nothing will be there to sell!"

Rain, rain, rain
Heavy rain,
Sometimes joy, sometime pain.

Over the radio,
A voice over the radio
"It's a tornado,
Stay away from your window!"

At first it was a little drizzle,
Wind against trees, sounds like a whistle,
Peering out a window, the eye of a couple,

Then up and down it goes again, water pouring from the sky.
Still without the water all the plants will die,
Saturated soil and at the side of the street a palm tree lies.

Water from the ground
A penny or a pound,
It must be a well that they found.

Rain, rain, rain,

Everywhere you turn, you will hear the same refrain
Rain, rain, rain
Heavy rain

Sometime joy and sometime pain

06/22/1998

The night of my arrest, I was at home with a good friend watching a game of basketball, after the game was over my friend wanted me to take him home, it was about midnight when the game finished, before I left to take my friend home I went into my son's room to see if he was sleeping which I always do.

Sometimes he would be sleeping other times he would not, I remember going into his room and seeing him sleeping on his stomach leaning down I pulled the cover up over him and kissed him good night. This was my oldest son; this would be the last time I saw him in his bed for the next twenty-three plus years.

My second son was not living with me at the time, I had saw him a few days earlier when I went to take him some stuff that I had bought for him. Whenever I would go to see him he would just run to me and it was heaven, he was different from his older brother in that he was full of energy, always have a line or two of sweat on the sides of his face.

These two baby boys was my world they meant the world to me, going to prison and not being able to do for them, to teach them and to be an example for them was pain beyond pain for me.

This poem is dedicated to them, I wrote it to say I am sorry, to apologise to them for not being there when they needed me most.

A FEW WORDS OF APOLOGY

A letter from ma daddy,
A letter from ma daddy,
A few words to a young "G"

Just a little baby when I first went away
Couldn't come to see you for a night or a day,
And even on your birthday,
To take you to a movie or to take you to a play.

A letter from ma daddy,
A letter from ma daddy,
A few words to a young "G"

Back in 1998 I got a letter from you mommy,
A tough little kid, she said you acted like me,

And when you had a flu,
Sleepless nights she had to go through.

Asthma,
She said you got it from your father,
And as you grew a little older,
How you got a little stronger.

Wish I could have taken you to a game of soccer,
And watched you clap your little hands
when your team scored a winner,
Shared a bag of popcorn and drank a soda.
And rested your little head upon ma shoulder,
Upon ma shoulder.

A letter from ma daddy,
A letter from ma daddy,
A few words to a young "G".

A real daddy, a real daddy.

Wish a could have been a real daddy,
To teach you how to swim and what to say to a lady,
How to write a letter, and how to tell a story,

A real daddy, a real daddy,
Wish I could have been a real daddy.

To watch you as you grow,
Watch you as you glow,
A lot about your young life, I am yet to know,
A life without your daddy was a heavy, heavy blow.

Never got to help you with your homework,
and when you had a test,
A smile nor a wink from your dad, you didn't get,
The letters that I wrote, I hope that you get,
A prayer to forgive and a prayer to forget.

A real daddy, a real daddy.
Wish a could have been a real daddy,
A real daddy.

Hope it's not too late,
For us to share a love so great,
For in my heart with destiny, I know we have a date.

And if I had another chance, on my life, I would bet
No need to worry, no need to fret,
A father's love you would sure to get.

A special love to each of you, my sons.
A special kind of love that will last as long as the sun,
Time spend, in laughter and fun

A real daddy
To teach them how to swim and what to say to a lady
A real daddy, a real daddy

12/08/2002

We were on solitary confinement; it was one month after the riot and the situation was getting from bad to worse. The guards were on a revenge binge, every day and every night they would come to our unit to intimidate us.

Some days they would strip us down to our underwear and T-Shirts and marched across the compound to the gym where we would be held for hours. This poem reflects those days-those experiences.

ONE OF THOSE DAYS

Life is not always what it seems,
Toss and turning in my dream,
Frustrated, angry want to scream.

As hard as the ground,
A pillow or a stone.
Sad and lonely, feeling all alone.

Have a book to read about the right way,
The wrong way,
But nothing changes it's the same every day.
Now I lay, upon this bunk I lay,

One of those days,
One of those days,
Now I lay, upon my bunk I lay.

The cock has yet to crow,
Still you could hear Massa voice coming to your door.

Then I said
As I scrambled out of bed,
"It must be the echoes from Massa voice,
which cause the pain in my head".

It was a bad day, I got the first hint,
As I made my way over to the sink,
It was my knee I hit that caused me to think,
I need a pen; I want some ink.

One of those days,
One of those days.

Looking out my door through a pane of glass,
Massa and his crew was about to serve the breakfast,
Food on the cart and I had to laugh,
I have the flu, it made me cough.

Two slices of white bread and peanut butter,
A spoon of coffee, and two packs of sugar.
So we ask, "Where is the hot water?"

Its days like these,
That makes one cry for ease.
Just a little cool breeze.

One of those days
One of those days

06/15/2012

I grew to love silence; in a way I had no choice, solitary
confinement was silent, I had to fall in love with my condition;
Be still became my mantra, I learned to listen, I developed
patience and I found inner strength.

BE STILL, BE STILL

The reason, the purpose,
Why men are made conscious?
Willing and serious?

Walking the path of the Martyr,
Walking without fear,
In the struggle you willingly share.

I set my sight on the mountain,
The summit of the mountain.

Then I climb
One step at a time,
A quiet space I seek to find
Searching for a new state of mind.

Be still, be still,
Dig down, deep within.
And just maybe you will find that hidden skill

Be still,
Dig down deep within.

Find self, it's universal,
Diverse, unique and special.

Then let go and just be,
Feel free,
And fly like a bird above a tree.

It a peace of mind,
Peace and tranquillity, I seek to find.

Had no need to live in fear,
All I had to do, give a listening ear,
Just a minute to show I really care.

So be still, be still,
And dig down deep within,
Finding that desire and will to live.

03/03/1999

A lesson I learned from my beloved mother, she always tell me to do unto others as I would want done unto me, this is an old saying which she lived by and so when I tried to explain what the word respect means to me, the most inclusive answer I could find was that old saying 'do unto other as you would want done unto you'

And so I wrote this poem from a place of wanted to be known as a person of high respect which meant I had to live a certain way; it was never all about me and what I want but it was the understanding that we are all interdependent and for there to be peace there must be mutual respect.

RESPECT, RESPECT;

Respect,
Respect,

They tell me your name is Respect,
That you give respect to who respect is due,
That in return respect is given you.

They say it's not about the money in your bank book,
The car that you drive or the way that you look.
It's all about the steps that you took,
Even after, a left jab or a right hook.

People watch the things you do,
They see in you,
Characteristics we only find in a few.

Respect,
Respect

They say it how you keep your word,
And the patience to wait your turn.
That makes you stand out in the crowd.

It's your manners at the dinner table,
Even a hard word, but you stayed humble.
The way you carry yourself, powerful, yet so simple.

Respect,
Respect,

They tell me, your name is called Respect.

They say you give respect to who respect is due,
That in return, respect is given to you.

Your name is called respect,
Time to the side you set,
Even if it means losing a bet.
From you a listening ear, a vulnerable kid will always get

For an helping hand, you're always there,
A side of you that tells the world how much you really care.
For even to a stranger, you willingly share.

Cool under pressure,
Never use words that could be considered
To be rude or out of order.

Its respect,
They say your name is Respect

02/30/2012

This poem was written out of my love for my culture and where I came from, it's about my coming to terms with the fact that what I was doing was leading to a dead-end road.

I had to change and when I did, good thing began to happen for me, CHANGE, CHANGE, CHANGE was written to encourage change.

CHANGE, CHANGE, CHANGE

Get out the word!
Get out the word!

East, West, North and South,

Get out the word!
Get out the word!

Change is not a word,
Feel it in your heart, feel it in your soul,
Is everything okay?
Okay!

Why worry, sitting around, looking out in space?
Get up! Move! And make haste!
Why worry about a case?
We have no time to waste.

A little rough around the edge,
Well, no time to beg.

A patch over here, a patch over there,
Still, no need to fear,
We are in this together, together we will bear.

It's okay, it's okay,
Time to try again,
Not every road is straight, sometime there is a bend.

Still, worry less,
If you look close enough, you will see
how much you are blessed.

Get out the word!
Get out the word!

East, West, North and South.

Change, change is not just a word,
Not just a word

Pick them up! Clear them out! Get a haircut!
Old closet! Close them up!
Nails cut!
Doors shut!
A new day,
Care less what others have to say,
Tomorrow will be different from today.
Give self a chance, find a new way!

Get out the word!
Get out the word!

This won't take long,
A little self-examination,
To make a few self-corrections.

In somethings we may fall, nothing wrong with that,
Back on your feet, strong and exact.

True that,
The war is over, the general is back!

Get up! Get out and move!
Get up, get out and move!

Change is not just a word,
Not just a word.

Get up!
Get out and move!

Change, Change, Change

Change is not just a word, not just a word.
Get up!
Get out and move!

07/11/2004

All I saw, was my physical self-image, just a reflection I write this poem from a place of growth and maturity. I was placed in an environment that forces me to see pass my physical self and finding that INNER MAN.

I learned and so this poem represent a process by which I began to listen to my conscience, that voice from within.

THE INNER MAN

As I make my way on life's path,
I sometimes struggle with my inner thoughts,
Even with my conscience, I often fought,
For in the vices of this world it seems I have bought.

With the lower self, the higher self must fight,
Fighting that inner battle for control of my appetite,
To protect myself from that which they say will shorten one's life,
A war within the inner man, even in the darkest of night.

Then I take a minute, for reflection,
A little meditation,
Seek that positive vibration,
Finding self-satisfaction.

So I open my eye and see, I open my ears and hear
For that inner man is always there,
A word of guidance, a voice that always cares

Drop the mic, drop the mic,
That inner voice,
Sometime stern, sometime nice,

Sincere, never hype,
A prototype.

Unique and special,
Universal,
That inner man, spiritual.
On our knees, on our knees,
Consequential.

That inner man, listen when he speaks,
It your safety, that he seek.

Loud and clear, Loud and clear,

No, stop! Don't go!
Not with him, don't go!
Still we go,
Now that inner voice we hear no more.

That inner man, that inner self,
Never need a whip, never need a belt,
Always feel free to say how he felt.
Listen carefully when that inner man speaks,
For it's your safety, that he seek,
Closer than a brother all your secret we will keep.

So take a minute, for reflection,
A little meditation,
Seek that positive vibration,
Finding self-satisfaction.

That inner man, that inner man,
Just a minute for reflection
Positive vibration.
Self-satisfaction

That inner man, that inner man

01/30/2013

This poem is one about an inner battle being fought between good and evil

IT'S A WAR OF ATTRITION

Psychology, philosophy, ideology
Ideals we wrestled with daily
A conflict within the mind
A war within man, his mind, soul and body

Searching for a state of consciousness
A desire to bring out the rest
Trying hard to be your best
Creating something in which to invest

Struggling against good and evil
A struggle that make some men humble

A war of attrition
Whether in the mind or on the battlefield
It's a war of attrition, a war of attrition
A time of great tribulation

Asymmetric in the Armageddon
The Armageddon
A war between the weak and the strong
Like nations, fighting against nation

When rape become a weapon
Famine, war and starvation
The movements of great population

Psychology, philosophy, ideology
Ideals we wrestled with daily
A conflict within the mind
A war within man, his mind, soul and body

The long walk, the trail of tears
Long lasting effects, even after 150 years
No one cares, no one cares

So they say they had a move to make
Essential steps to take
like the dough to make a cake
In the oven, the innocents are left to bake

The war of attrition
Asymmetric in the Armageddon

04/05/1999

I wrote this poem from a place of pain, yet hope and certainty, I had a high degree of hope; hope that one day I would be freed from the halls of captivity. Freedom oh freedom is a cry from what we saw as the belly of the breast.

FREEDOM, OH FREEDOM

Ideals we hold still,
The freedom to think, think as we will,
Freedom to work, even at a mill,
Freedom to be restless, freedom to be still.

Freedom to speak, speak our minds,
Freedom to a meal, come, come lets us dine,
Freedom to space, freedom to time,
I will respect yours, please respect mine.

Freedom to take an endeavor,
To take the job you prefer,
Enjoying the fruits of your labor.

Freedom to go, go where-ever,
Freedom to come, come together,
To take a stair or to climb a ladder.

Freedom to one, freedom to all,
Freedom to play, run the track, or kick a ball,
Freedom stand, stand tall.
And if you fall?
Get up we say! Its humanity's call!

Freedom to do,
Freedom for you,
Still remembering, it's not just you.

Freedom of expression,
A right for everyone,
A right that will bring peace and understanding across our land.

Freedom, Oh freedom!
Sweet freedom!

These ideals we hold still,
Freedom to think, think as we will,
Freedom to be restless, freedom to be still.

Freedom! Oh freedom!
Sweet freedom!

01/10/2003

This is one of those poems where dreams and imaginary desires seems to meet, still poem came from a place within, a place where dreams were real and where my imagination held my focus.

WHITE DRESS, WHITE DRESS

White dress, white dress, she wore a white dress,
It was an evening gown; she was dressed to impress.

This was my umpteen time in the hornet's nest,
And never in my wildest dream, would I have guessed,
In a place like that I would have found my empress.

A delight for my eyes to see, upon her
face my attention came to rest,
Like a ray in a sunset,
A gift that the Gods had left,
And a blessing that took my breath.

Then slowly as I regain my composure,
A word of peace as she got a little closer,
A greeting she return that made me wonder.

Couldn't help wanting to take her out for dinner,
And having a conversation over a glass of chilled coconut water,
Stuffed crab and smoked lobster.

So, I said, "hi, don't I know you?'
To which she replied, excuse me, do you know me?"
"And where would you have met me?"

Her response had a touch of uncertainty,
I could see
She wanted more from me.

Making it up as I go,
I told her, I saw her a month ago,
And how I loved her flow.

In her eyes, she held my stare, doing so,
My mind was blown,
Then a song came on that stole the show,
Right there and then, I knew, she knows'
On the dance floor, we had to go.

So, I took her hand,
Willingly, she let me take her hand.
A sign to let me know she understand,
We were about to start a dance, which would last all night long.

Confident and sure,
I took her to the dance floor,
Then as we dance, the music began to pierce our inner core,
To our soul, it seems the DJ had found a door.
With each song, we were crying out for more.

So, as we dance the night away.
In each other arms we dared to stay,
And there we stayed.

In our hearts, if only for a day.
Then we dreamt to lay,

White dress, white dress,
She wore a white dress,
It was an evening gown; she was dressed to impress.

04/16/2013

One of my first poems, the 'ESSENCE OF LOVE' started that set of poem where dreams and imagination meet. I was in search for hope in what was a series of lost and pain; this poem provided the space for me to let go and find peace. It was therapeutic.

THE ESSENCE OF LOVE

When my thoughts take me away from my present reality,
I am on an island surrounded by the deep blue sea,
Where the scent of rose and exotic plants tells the story,
A story of a nearing spring.

Then I find myself in the bliss of love,
The ultimate bliss of love.

I see her beautiful eyes, I see her smile,
Side by side,
That special someone, she never leaves my side

Then I am overwhelmed by her nearness,
In the essence of love, for she was blessed,
Desiring for her, I could care less.

In my thoughts, we were dancing to the tune of jazz,
The Mississippi blues, the reggae bass line.
To the sweet sounds of Mo town, Smoky
Robinson, the Supremes,
R&B, Stevie Wonder.

In the essences of love,
Traveling under the stars from above,

To a place of rest, like a pair of doves,
Where together we fit like a pair of gloves.

To her I made a promise, that I would be careful and tender,
For she was to be my other,
Making sweet music together,
Having a bite for lunch and sharing in a late super,

In my heart, I am with her and she is with me,
In the essence of love where we hope to be,
Remaining for eternity.

12/02/1998

I wanted to tell you about my world, but it was hard to find words to express the true essence of where I was at that time in my journey. It was easier for me to tell you about my condition by talking about my hope and dreams of see the free world again, this poem was a cry for freedom.

YOUR WORLD, NOT MY WORLD

How I wish to see your world,
Not my world,
To see your world, not my world.

Sounds of rain, rain drop,
Beating down on my roof top,
Stop, stop.

Then a ray of sun comes shining through,
How I wish, somewhere to go, something to do.

Wishing I could see the ancient city of Petra,
Another world wonder,
The Serengeti, in the wilds of Tanzania,
To see lions or the dangerous eyes of a tiger.

The horn of Africa,
On the banks of river Kwanza,
To see the great walls of China,
The Blue Mountain Peak of Jamaica.

How I wish to see your world,
Not my world,
Your world, not my world,

The Eiffel Tower of Paris,
The Pyramids of Egypt,
A day at Disney,
Yellow Stone Park, out in the open country,
To see the capital city of Sidney.

How I wish to see,
How I wish to see,
Just to be.

A day in your world,
Not my world,
Your world, not my world.

Just one day in your world, not my world.

05/026/2009

I wrote this poem in the middle of my transition I had begun to learn and to understand purpose, I had started to forgive myself. This poem is about taking ownership of who I am and seeing the best in yourself,

THE MIRROR

Mirror, oh mirror,
Yesterday, today and tomorrow,
I see time, I see a future,
Out in open space a reflection like a picture.

Never telling the full story,
It's only a physical reflection of who you may be.

Who could tell?
But it won't matter,
Because, a picture,
Is just a picture.

Looking shy,
Then rumours fly,
An unkind image staring in your eye,
Makes you want to cry,
Wishing only to die.

Then I asked:

Is that image, all there is to see about me?
What part of it represent the family tree?

Mirror, oh mirror.

How could a simple reflection be?
The full essence of me?

Unique and special, I am more then what the eyes can see
No one knows the potential that lies within me.
This is something the mere eyes can never see.

Dedication, and discipline
I reach deep within
Grabbing hold of purpose, aim or a day in the gym,
The true me,
Is me,
A reflection is only a tiny bit of me.

Mirror, oh mirror.

04/07/2007

This poem represent a thinking where we have a responsibility to treat each other with more care and consideration. What I was experiencing at that time were guards who saw us as animals, even if not consciously; subconsciously they were treating us as if we were not human beings.

MAN, OH MAN was written seven months after the riot that left one guard dead and many more seriously wounded. This was a time of reprisal; guards saw us as the enemies and treat us as such, our treatment were brutal.

MAN, OH MAN

Father, brother, uncle, son,
Whether joy, pain or fun.
Through your hands the affairs of the world shall run

In the beginning the Creator, created man,
To him, He gave dominion.
Subdue the land,
And when you have a son, teach him
well, that he may understand,
The love of God, and everyone upon the land.

Remember he said, I know your ways oh man,
At times, you fail to understand,
Great mischief you have made upon the land.

The blood of Abel, you have left along life's path,
Sometimes you speak well, words from your heart,
Then again, for what? So many wars you have start.

Rush and haste
Have made your hands, hands of waste,
Against you, the angels have made a case.
In the hot seat, they demand to see your face.

They say it's not about your pretty looks,
It's about the millions of lives that you took,
Drop the bomb! Drop the bomb! The earth shook!

This is not a hook,
Its reality, hidden in the pages of your book,

Man, oh man,
Man, oh man.

What evil you have brought upon mankind?
Over time,
So much strife, war, and crime,

Now death is at your doorsteps,
Over you the angels wept,
Your words you gave, but your words, you never kept.

The truth, you have taken for a mockery,
Filling your pockets with the people's money,
Your laughs and smiles are all phony.
Your actions are crimes against humanity.

All over the world,
Are signs of the many lies you have told,
Pollution in the air, where it was once warm, now ice cold,

So much power we have given you,
And of all the things you could do.
You oppressed the poor until their hands are black and blue.

Man, Oh man.
Man, Oh man.

02/12/2011

This is a poem, attempt to bring awareness to the issue relating to the eroding of our coastline. This poem give voice to the need for us to take care of what nature has given us in the beauty and vastness of our universe.

THE SHRINKING SANDS

Stand and watch and you will see,
Where the coral reefs once be,
Now shrinking sand is all there is to see.

Iceland, Greenland,
Ice caps no more stand.
The ice is melting in a faraway land.

Where once lay sheets of ice,
Where polar bears of the wild play nice,
Now a sight of melting ice.

A whistling sound above a tree,
The whistling sounds of a jet ski
As a touring couple, race across the calm blue sea.

Against the coral reefs the waves will slam,
Sheets of white corals, to the sea floor they land.
Then as I walked the sandy shores,
I could feel tiny grains of sand betwixt my toes.
As I watch a fisherman row his boat to shore

Up the Atlantic coast,
Into the Gulf of Mexico,
Wherever the wind will blow.

Cities that once glowed,
Cities of light no mo'

Stand and watch, you will see
Where the Coral reefs once be,
Now shrinking sand is all there is to see.

Bring tears to my eyes,
If nothing is done our coral reefs will die.

Stand and watch, you will see,
Where the Coral reefs once be,
Now shrinking sand is all there is to see.

15/04/2010

It was difficult writing this poem, here I was telling a story about my own experience growing without my father, not knowing him and how much I had dreamt of seeing him walking in my door, yet I knew this poem was about my sons who were growing without their father and how painful that must have been for them.

A poem for all our young boys, young boys who are today growing up without a father to call dad. SOMEBODY PLEASE TELL ME; is a call to men who has fathered a child and for whatever reason had not been around lately to see how that child is doing to turn around and go back to that child giving that child someone to depend on.

SOMEBODY PLEASE TELL ME

Somebody please tell me,
Somebody please tell me,

Is there a father out there?
A dad who really cares?
One to hug a little boy and wipe away a tear?

A lonely little boy, at the tender age of nine
Deep in thoughts, in his little mind
A goal he set, his dad he seeks to find.

With his sad little face, staring out his window
Day after day watching as too and fro,
The neighbours go.

Wondering if his dad will ever show,
For the face of his dad he really didn't know.

Where is my dad? He often wondered,
A word game he sometimes played as he stared out yonder.
Is he my dad, or just another stranger?
Growing up with a single mother,
A dream he has to find his father

Somebody please tell me,
Somebody please tell me,

Is there a father out there?
A dad who really cares.
One to hug a little boy and wipe away a tear?

Tell me if you are sure,
That tonight his dad would come walking through his door,
To give him the taste of a father's love, one to last forever more.
A kind of daddy's love, touches his inner core,
Just a moment to let him know he will
have his dad forever more.

To every father out there we must make the case.
Hurry on home, no more time to waste.
Come on home to take the sadness from that little boy's face,
Leaving him happy, and full of grace.
A father's love every child would take.

Give the little man a dad, someone to call a friend,
A dad on whom he could depend.
It's time to heal the breach, a tender little heart to mend.

Somebody please tell me,
Somebody please tell me,

Is there a father out there?
A dad who really care.
One to hug a little boy and wipe away a tear?

Somebody please tell me,
Somebody please tell me.

Is there a dad out there?
Who for a little boy has some time to spare?
To show a young son the love of a dad who really cares.

Somebody please tell me,
Somebody please tell me,

Is there a dad out there?

Somebody please tell me
Somebody please tell me

08/05/2013

Looking back, 2013 was the year when the institution was easing up on what had been emergency control of the institution since the riot of 2012. This emergency order kept the entire population of more than 2000 restricted to our cells. For some of us this was overwhelming and psychologically draining.

This poem reflects a mind-set of survival; even if they would kill me physically, I would still survive because I AM HISTORY AND HISTORY IS ME

HISTORY IS ME

I am history, and history is me.

For I came in the genes of my people,
Mothers and fathers, born wise and humble.

And so, through me they live.
And through my children and through their seeds I live.

Lock me in a cage and throw away the key,
Still I am history and history is me,
Doing remarkable things before, then and after you saw me.

Out of darkness, the sun to rise, the sun to set and the sun to be,
As the moon, the stars, and the mountains stand above the sea,
And a drop of rain, let you plant a tree.
So is history and history is me

Millions of year ago, they say we were on our hands and knees.
But today an upright man, to stand before eternity,
Building and creating for our posterity.

The books we wrote,
From them the world will quote,

About a time that passed,
Through our children, history will blast,
A story we tell that will forever last.

So, I am history,
And history is me.

11/11/2009

I wrote this poem in honour of the Sandy Hook school Elementary Shooting in Newtown Connecticut USA. This mass shooting touches my heart, I could not believe a person could be so cold bloodied as to do such an evil act.

I cried for those children and all our children who are at risk and vulnerable to street crime, youth violence and yes wanton violence such as the one at Sandy Hook.

ECHOES, ECHOES

Echoes in my ears, tears in my eyes.
Who will pay the price for the innocent cries?

Echoes, echoes.

Echoes in my ears, tears in my eyes,
Who will pay the price for the innocent cries?

Who will pay the price for the innocent cries, in my dreams?
I see faces, I hear screams.

In my head, I feel a thumping in my head,
In my bed, I roll over on my bed,
There it was, twenty children lay dead.

Grief and fear, it touches the soul,
The human soul,
Still half the story is yet to be told.

M16, AK47 gun clips,
Extra clips,

Did they miss this?
Laws on the books, how could they miss this?

High school, college, university,
Kindergarten, even elementary,
He had no sense of reality,
His weapons he empty.

So, it seem
It was a killing team,
Stillness yet you could hear the children scream.

Echoes in my ears, tears in my eyes,
Who will pay the price for the innocent cries?

Echoes, echoes,

Echoes in my ears, tears in my eyes,
Who will pay the price for the innocent cries?

National Rifle Association flush with money,
Members of Congress they spend to lobby.

Mr President, can you hear me?
Do you see the Commercials on TV?

Too much guns, guns control,
Your role, my role,
Who else was told?

Echoes in my ears, tears in my eyes,
Who will pay the price for the innocent cries?

Echoes, echoes,

A gun just fire,
Someone pulled the trigger,

Children running for cover,
A teacher, even a caretaker.

Nowhere to run, nowhere to hide,
Got to get outside,
And catch me a ride.

School bus, bus stop, carjack,
Have you seen him?
Kidnapped, hijacked,
Have you seen him?

Echoes in my ears, tears in my eyes,
Who will pay the price for the innocent cries?

Echoes, echoes,

Echoes in my ears, tears in my eyes,
Who will pay the price for the innocent cries?

30/01/2013

This poem is for you the reader to see in his or her own way, I wrote it from what was going on in my mind; I was in search of a place of peace.

IT'S A SHADOW

It's a shadow,
A shadow,
A shadow.

Darkness covers, hearts quiver,
Living among the trees, a shadow.

Lucky me, the night had crossed the day,
Dawn was still a distant mile away.

Crystal dew covered the open field,
Glistening like a shield,
Over the evergreen,

A long the ridge line,
I made my way over to a cluster of pine trees.

Trees that stand tall like towers, towering into the night,
With weary knees, tired legs, sleepy eyes,
It seems the night had passed me by.

Then in the cluster of trees,
I looked, looking for a place to rest my tired legs,
For it was said,
Betwixt the trees one could find a place to rest his sleepy head.

So I looked, and woe,
I saw a shadow.

Cries echoed,
I saw a shadow,
A shadow, a shadow.

Like a glare of light,
To the eye a great delight,
A glance to the right,
And there it was in plain sight.

Then a glance to the left, a stare up ahead,
To the place I wish to make my bed,
But there it was, like a living dead.

A shadow,
A dark figure,
Then I wondered,

Living among the trees, a shadow?
I saw a shadow,
My heart quivered.

Living amongst the trees, I saw a shadow,
A shadow,
A shadow.

04/12/2011

I saw him just like I saw any other person, he was just another prisoner sent to be my cell-mate, oh was I wrong, from the very first day he came into my cell people was saying this guy had mental issues.

Growing up, I was petrified of persons with mental illness, talking to the young man you would not know he was sick, except for the occasional silent treatment he seems ok to me, when I would cook I would save some for him.

I tried to be his friend, we get along very well for the more than six months that he live in the cell, we got along well until one night when I woke up to find him stand next to my bunk starting down at me.

Waking up to find him staring down at me was the most petrifying moment of all my 23 years of captivity. The very next morning I asked for him to leave my cell, which the counsellor at first did not want to do. HE JUST STOOD THERE is one of those poems that are based on one of my many experiences over the many years behind the bars of captivity.

HE JUST STOOD THERE

His world was on his shoulder,
He stared out yonder,
Made me wonder,
Could my life be in danger?

Eyes empty and cold,
Lips between his teeth, tightly folded
By himself in his own little world,

Diamond or gold?
Whatever he had someone must have stolen.

Out in space,
He stood there staring out in space,
When he moved, he moved with focus and grace.
Step by step, each step at a steady pace,
No need for rush, no need to haste,

Sometimes I wondered, what he could be thinking,
The empty look in his eyes, what message was he sending?
Made me wished the door was opened.

And even though I could sleep,
And his language I did not speak,
For each other's language, they didn't teach,
Running away would be a sign, that I was weak.

Then from side to side as he glanced
Why with my life did they take this chance?
For in an instance,
Any moment at me he could have pranced.

Once a friend I asked,
What's wrong with him, why he rarely talks?
The answer came that he used to talk,
He used to laugh,
But now he walks,
Alone he walks,
Like a predator, his prey he stalks.

Someone said, he must be crazy
A brother, a sister or it could have been his lady,
He must have lost his baby.

He got a letter,
It came from his mother,
Every word that he uttered,
You could feel the pressure.

He got a little louder,
Made me wonder,
And take a stand like a soldier.

Six feet tall,
Six feet tall,

There he stood facing the wall.
The strong will stand, the weak will fall
I heard a sound, someone must have called,
I saw his head; he banged his head against the wall.

Tough time,
Like a mountain to climb,
Once a life of champagne and crime,
Now it seems he had lost his mind.

There he stood,
If only he could,
But only a few really would.

So much pain, If only he could,
With a sound mind, go back to his hood,
For the youth, to do some good.

But he just stood there,
Staring out yonder,
For his world was on his shoulder,

17/02/2014

Had to go down deep within to find words, meaningful words to motivate and inspire strength and hope. Hard climb are words defines the path I had to travel during those early days of my struggle.

HARD CLIMB

It's a hard climb,
Such a hard climb.

Few have made it to the top,
A journey few will ever forget.

How I wish I had a bike or a car,
Then the journey would not seem so far.

My legs, oh my back,
The weight so heavy, like a knapsack.

The sole my feet, my legs,
No matter what was said
I am too proud to beg,

So many nights away from my bed,
Thought I had a need to be fed
With the task ahead
Take the lead, not waiting to be led
With the task ahead,

To cross a slope and a valley out yonder,
A water hole and a tree for shelter.

It's the end of winter
Summer is just around the corner
We won't have to wait much longer

Get this task done one way or another

It's a hard climb,
Such a hard climb.

Still, still we persevere

Hard climb,
Such a hard climb.

15/01/1999

A poem designed to inspire faith and to express trust and belief in a power outside of one's self.

TO THE GODS I PRAY

To the Gods I pray,
To the Gods I pray,

Teach me how, when and what to say.

So long a life you have given me,
More than many who have passed away.
A life I have tried to live in a humble way,
Sometimes work and sometimes play.

To the Gods I pray,
To the Gods I pray,

Give me a mind to understand,
A heart that lets me fear no other man.

Hands of courage that makes me strong,
Feet to make me stand,
Or even to walk miles across the land.

Thanks be to thee,
A table you have prepared for me,
As I stand before my enemy.

Clothes on my back,
A place to lay back,
Away for a while but now I am back.

Some may fret and some may worry,
Going through life in a rush and a hurry,
A life we have lived, more rewarding than many.

A great blessing you have given me.
Long life and prosperity.

Through so many struggles you have held me down,
Holding my feet firm to the ground,
Standing up or laying down.

Whether on a couch, or up in a chair,
Your love and care,
Always there.

From whence you come no one knows,
Wherever the wind may blow,
There your power flow.

This I know and this I understand,
The sun that shines and the rain that falls upon the land,
All are blessings from your mighty hand.
Breathe from your nostrils and the work of your hands
With a simple act, from dust you have created man.

So to the Gods I pray,
To the Gods I pray,
Giving me the wisdom and knowledge if even for a day,
Teach me how, when and what to say.

To the Gods I pray,
To the Gods I pray,
Teach me how, when and what to say.

To the Gods, I pray

26/03/2006

I grew up in a time when the abuse of women by men was an open secret accepted and part of our culture. Women were looked upon more as male property than unique persons and individuals, fellow human beings deserving of equal treatment and due respects.

The patriarchal norms and culture that has rule since the dawn of time has produce men who believe in the physical and mental abuse of women. This poem refers to a woman who had, had enough so SHE WALKS not knowing where she was going or what the future holds, she took her life and future into her hands and so, SHE WALKS!

SHE WALKS SHE WALKS

Like a work of art,
She walks.
"Where now, what will I do?" She asked.

"The road is wide, the road is long,
How was I so wrong?"

Where next?
Where next?
She wonders, as she walks,
As she walks.

As she walks, she smiles, she talks to herself,
It's a beautiful day, beautiful thoughts.
In her eyes you could see, like a faraway star they beam,
Even though overwhelmed, still her eyes they gleam.

A smile, a laugh,
"What next?"
"What next?"
She asks.

A park, a show, a home by a pond or spring, a place of peace.
It's serenity that she seeks,
As she walks, in her mind she speaks.

Then a voice, she hears a voice, "here, here,
Over here."

A voice so deep and far away, at first, she did not know,
Then she listens

I heard that voice before,
She was sure.

"Here, here over here."
She stops, in her tracks she stops.

Memories, she remembers, floods of memories, it's him.
That sparkle in her eyes, the star like beam, that beautiful glare,
Now they fades, no more there,
Yes, she stares.

In a distant space, she stares,
So many years, so many years,
So many tears, so many tears,

So many memories
She remembers, flood of memories.

Lines, wrinkles, a scar, bags under her eyes.
So heavy, she cries, yes she cries,
"Oh my, oh my."
A cry so loud it reaches the sky.

Hands around her neck,
Hands so soft, his touch she melts,

Snuggled in his arms
So strong and powerful his arms.

A tower of strength he used to be,
In his eye she used to look, a place of security she used to see.

Every friend who saw them told her, he was the one,
Not long,
Will you take this man?

"Yes, I do, yes, I do."

On an island in the sun,
Kisses and caress, so much fun.

In his bosom where she lays
Sounds of love, sounds of play, foreplay.
Soon a set of twins was on the way,
What else, what else was there to say?
In his arms she dreamed to stay.

Then one day, she sees,

Then she asks, could this really be?
Because in him a different man she began to see.

Home for dinner will you come?
From his lips a response did not come.

But in his eyes anger sets,
Could it be, did he ask about her dress?
For him she wore that dress.

Up in her face he came, kissed and caressed,
She thought,
But into her heart like a dart.

So fast,
Like a bomb blast,
His right hand across her face,
A place she thought was safe.

Then it was his hands around her neck,
Pressing so hard into her flesh,
So hard fingerprints, he left.

"Here, here over here."

But she walks,
Yes, she walks.

She wipes her eyes, dries her tears,
Someone new, someone who will truly care.
The road is wide, the road is long a path she once fears,

Oh dear,
She thought, does anyone really care?

"What next?"
"What next?"

She asks,
As she walks,
As she walks.

A park, a show, a home by a pond, a place of peace,
It's serenity that she seeks.

Now she walks,
Yes, she walks.

Like a work of art,
Yes, she walks.

02/06/1997

I heard and read about stories that brought fear and trepidation, this poem was a warning; preparing me for what I was about to face. THE STORIES I HAVE HEARD, speak of the unknown and its realities.

THE STORIES, I HAVE HEARD

As I walk, I hang my head,
For I know not what might have become of me.

The stories that I have heard, tells tales of no return,
They tell tales of men who over time
Have lost their minds.

The stories I have heard tell tales,
Of days, days so dark, dark as the midnight,
Where signs of hope are nowhere in sight.

The stories,
The stories.

So I hang my head, fear was at my door,
The smiling sun I saw no more.

The heat of summer,
There, warmth to acquire,
Yet I shiver.
From the top of my head to the tip of my toes,
I shiver.

Gates locked,
Roads blocked,
So I hang my head,
For I knew not what danger lies ahead.

So they say, few ever get to see the sun again,
The toughest of minds, it is designed to bend,
They say you may know someone, but not to call a friend.

The stories, the stories,
The stories that I have heard.

30/11/2010

Had a friend in mind when I wrote this poem, I dedicated it her, I member the joy that came over me seeing her smile when the doctor told her the baby was a boy, it's a boy she heard the doctor say

IT'S A BOY

On her back she lay,
It's a boy
She heard the doctor say.

As she lay,
On her back she lay.
It's a boy,
She heard the doctor say.

Tears down the sides of her face,
Hearing those words were not a normal case,
Food to eat but she had lost her taste.

Never married before,
He was the first to walk through her door.
She knew no other man; with him she was sure.

Promises of love, happiness and a family,
A promise that made her dreamt of having his baby,
A healthy little baby.

In each other's hearts love was set,
In him her desires were met.
Sharing all they had, having no regret,
Lots of love and passionate sex.

And that they did,
Yes, they did
Desire for a child, a dream she never hide.
Birth control to stop her from having that kid,
No, no, pills she never did.

Yes, I do, yes, I do.
They made that vow
In each other arms, they bowed.

Three months later, time had run so fast,
It was Sunday morning and they were having a blast
Then just after breakfast,
She returned from the bathroom with a funny little laugh,
Staring in her face he had to laugh,
He knew she wanted to talk.

In his arms, she whispered to him,
Now he too was laughing,
The news of a child she was carrying.

Good news, over names they laugh and talked,
Then back to the bedroom where they walked

A happy way
To start the day,
To each other, a lot they had to say,
A word of prayer because they always prayed.

Then talk was over it was time to play,
In each other arms there they lay,
And they lay.

Two months later,
She fell in the shower,
She had to see a doctor,
Sorry the doctor said, we found blood on the cover.

A little boy, no a little girl,
Which to her would have meant the world.
More precious than diamond or pearl.

A perfect marriage,
Now a miscarriage,
No one know how she would manage.

Pain and fear,
In him she found a friend one who really cared
For in her pain she knew he would willingly share.

He felt her pain,
To her he had to make it plain,
Staying in bed was vain,
There was nothing for us to gain.

I have a plan,
I bought a caravan,
Forget your pain and let me take your hand.

I have a plan,
I bought a caravan.

At first, she did not care, she couldn't understand.
Then with her bags in her hand,
She let him take her hand,
And off they went, to tour the land.

One year later and there she lay,
On her back she lay,

It's a boy,
She heard the doctor say.

As she lay,
On her back she lay,

It's a boy,
She heard the doctor say.

13/10/2011

A poem written to our young people caught up in the culture of gangs and youth violence. Designed to inspire and motivate a new mind-set, a new attitude towards their future and wellbeing. STOP THE GUN PLAY calls on our youth to put down their weapons and open the books.

STOP THE GUN PLAY

This is not a word game that we play
I say,
Stop the gun play,
And save a young life on the way.

Brothers and sisters getting murdered every day,
In the streets, every kid wants an AK.
Gun shots, gun play,
On the street side another lifeless body lay.

In the streets of London,
A group or a gang,
Another youngster running with a knife in his hand.

I say
Put your knives away,
And stop the gun play,
This is not a word game that we play.

Tell the youths what's right,
Show them how to stop a fight
Before the loss of another precious young life,
Fatherless children, a widow or a wife.

A mother knows the sound of a child's helpless cry,
It's not a matter of hope or a question of why?

In front of a jury, a killer will sweat,
Lawyers before the judge, motion set
On the killer's chance people place their bet,
While a mother and a father mourns an innocent child's death.

Who will win?
Who will win?
Once prince, a young king,
Now a killer charge with killing a future king.

Gun shots, gun play,
Well then, what else is there for us to say?

I say
Stop the gun play,
This is not a word game that we play.
Gun shots, gun play,

Drop your knives and put your guns away,
And save a young life on the way.

Gun shot, gun play,
Drop your knives and put your gun away,
And save a young life on the way

Peace.

24/01/2013

From the east to the west, north to the south, whether push or pull; populations' people are on the move; braving serious injury, jail, imprisonment and even death, men women and children leaving their homeland in search of a better life.

This poem THE FROM WHENCE I CAME; is about the complexity behind the reasons why families are fleeing their homeland for the unknown.

THE LAND WHENCE I CAME

Traveling night and day, searching for a moment in the sun,
For the land whence, I came,
A land from where to run.

War and famine, wine or rum,
Lands to farm but nothing is done.
No time for school, no time for fun.

The land whence I came,
Constant struggle, constant pain.

Rivers, springs, oceans and seas
Hills to climb, beaches to see,
Rivers and streams flowing endlessly.

Look and you will see,
Wealth within its soil, even under a tree,
How could it be?
In such a place, the people live in perpetual poverty.

The land whence I came,
Constant struggle, constant pain.

Why did I, why so many of us?
To save our lives, run we must,
For power and control, the leaders fight and fuss.

The least of issue, they run to their little corner,
Plotting and planning death for each other.
The wealth of the land they seek to plunder.

The wellbeing of the people doesn't matter,
Twenty children, blindfolded and murdered,
Twenty-five found dead in a dumpster.

Running into people's homes without a question ask,
On a mission, a made-up task,
Killing everything in sight, leaving a pet cat for last.
Wickedness prevail, no lessons from the past.

The land whence I came,
Constant struggle, constant pain.

Ancient scrolls and artefacts,
Crated and box,
Off across the seas never to come back.

Massive of people living in shock,
While the leaders lay back,
Drinking whiskey on the rock.

For the massive, hard nights, hard days,
Still the leaders of the land go about their lives unfazed.
To each other high fives and high praise.

Living a life of splendour,
Speeding out in Benz and shiny Range Rover,
Not far away, just around the corner,
A sick old man looking for food and shelter.

The land whence I came,
Constant struggle, constant pain.

Traveling night and day, searching for a moment in the sun,
For the land whence, I come,
A land from where to run.

War and famine, wine and rum,
Lands to farm but nothing is done,
No time for school, no time for fun.

The land whence I came,
Constant struggle, constant pain.

04/04/2004

The homies, the homies is a poem that highlights the lies about gang loyalty; how RIP and "I will be there for you to the end" are just words.

In reality, very little loyalty exists with criminal gang members and even more, few gang members stay loyal to the degree that they willing provide a helping hand to the fallen member or to the family of that member who end up behind bars facing life in prison.

THE HOMIES, THE HOMIES

They have a brother in a pen.
It's time like these when a rebel needs a friend.

Never knew the day would have come,
When from the battlefield the homies would leave run,
Leaving a soldier, like a brother or a son,
To fight alone until the war is done.

So much history, so much fun,
Eating a meal or chewing a gum,
Wherever you see one, the other will soon come.

Shipping fees,
Living off the seas,
Stacking cheese,
Money in their pockets, so they live at ease.

Down to the beach to get a little cool breeze,
Out to the movies
At your side, the homies never leave.

General they use to say, when we sat upon the throne,
Now locked in a cage, far away from home,
The homies are nowhere to be found.

Every month you hear the homie have new telephone,
Digits from the homie, but none to be found,
From the homies not a word nor a sound.

Has all the homies forget,
But how could they forget?
What about the standards that were set?
Where every rebel deserved respect.
On the homies we use to bet,
A losing card, in their hearts it was set.
Nothing was there for us to get.

Now I sit and wonder,
Were the homies friends, foes are something other,
Just a thought to consider,
Then again does it really matter?

Taken off the battlefield,
The fate, of a soldier was sealed
Hypocrites will run, before enemy they will kneel,
Hands out looking for a deal.

The rights of a soldier, they seek to steal,
Can the wounded heart of a soldier ever heal?

The rich will live, survival for the strong,
Who is right or who is wrong,
In the pen, is there an innocent man?
The guilty must pay, the law of the land.

When the indictment came,
And they saw your name,
The law was plain,
Someone was about to feel some pain.

Alone the guilty will stand,
Hoping to find a helping hand,
A familiar face, or an inspiring one.

Gone were the days, of the glory and fame,
Rip, Rip, but none to share the pain,
A call went out, what was the aim?

Well,
They have a brother in a pen,
The homies, the homies

They have a brother in a pen,
Time like those when a rebel needs a friend.

The homies, the homies

06/06/2000

When you find a person you can really trust to call a friend you can truly count yourself bless.

A GOOD FRIEND IS HARD TO FIND

Like a lion to tame, a mountain to climb,
A good friend is hard to find.
A relationship, where with kindness bind.

To lend a hand,
A shoulder to cry on,
Just to show you understand.

Befriend a stranger,
It might just be you have found a brother,
Or a sister.

Take heed,
A good friend is a blessing, a blessing indeed.
Take your time, no need to speed,
A good friend is all you need.

Of all the many people we meet,
Only a few, for friendship we keep.
One to share the pain and one to take the heat,
Up for a friend he willingly speak.

A simple smile, or a word of praise,
A friend's hope one seeks to raise.

Just spend a little time,
Run this through your mind,
Even though at first a stranger, now it
seems a friend for a lifetime.

A lion to tame, a mountain to climb,
A good friend is hard to find.

A lion to tame, a mountain to climb,
A good friend is hard to find.

13/08/2011

The social interactions between peoples are the building blocks of society and the nature of humanity. Relationships are about understanding and sharing each other's pain and aspiration.

RELATIONSHIPS

When a tragedy could be just a blink away,
Our relationships should be here to stay.
For a good relationship there aren't enough words to say.

Relationships with family and friends,
So let us build them,
Keep them,
Like a chain link fence, let us link them.

It's all about you need me and I needing you,
Together there are so much more we could do.

Upon each other, we could depend,
And even if I never see you again,
Relationships of just family and friends.
So let us build them and keep them.

Shared values, conduct and respect,
Whatever you give, in return you will get,
Relationships lost; relationships set.

Whether social, business or intimate,
No need to worry, no need to fret,
If it's raining outside, you sure to get wet.

Say what you may, do what you will,
And still!

In the end, no man stand alone,
You could be living in a palace or simple home,
A king, a peasant or clown.

Good, bad or indifferent,
Good bad or indifferent,
Relationships with family and friends,
Like a chain link fence, link them.

01/06/2013

This is the sound I heard when they came to extract one of us they think were not following the rules.

But its more than the sound you hear during these extractions, it's the reality that one of us was getting beat down by guards who was the law; judge, jury, and executioner.

TAP, TAP, TAP

It's quiet now, so quiet, not a sound, oh!
Wait, a door,
A squeaking door,
A squeaking door.

Footsteps, footsteps,
Like music, tap dancing,
Tap, tap, tap; tap, tap, tap.
Someone is coming.

People, they are coming,
Like an army, they are coming,
Marching on to war, war with who?
Maybe you.

It's quiet now, so quiet,
Not a sound, oh!
Wait, a shout!
Someone is shouting.

An angry shout,
So where about,
A scream, someone is screaming.

Footsteps, stop! Open up!
Tap, tap, tap,
Tap, tap, tap,
Footsteps, stop! Open up!

I hear the sound,
I hear the sound,
But no one is to be found,
No one around.

Then a scream, someone is screaming,
Someone is bawling,

Oh no, oh no,
Could it be, could it be?

Tap-tap-tap,
Tap-tap-tap,
Footsteps stopped.

Open up1
Tap, tap, tap,
Tap, tap, tap,

Footsteps,
Stop! Open up!
Its quiet now, so quiet, not a sound,
Not a sound.

10/09/2009

This poem is all about sharing, a formal accusation against those that have it all but neglect to share even with a person who has nothing, not even food.

GIVE A LITTLE

What is there for us to do?
When the wealth of the world is in the hands of a few,
An empty plate is left for me and you.

Who is the big boss?
The question was asked
Quickly an answer came, not so fast.

Still pain and hunger across my face,
Rush and haste,
No they say, slow your pace.

Then I dream,
Yes I dream, for it seem,
Over their eyes someone has cast a beam.

Their feet they drag,
Over their riches they brag,
With a scarlet letter, the poor they tag.

Tired of being shoved and shuffled,
To the back of the line to crumble,
Make space I say, for me at the table.

So long I have waited, making myself humble,
Hoping to get a little,
To satisfy the desires of the people.

Just a little,
Yet those that has it all
Sees no reason, they are not trouble
By seeing others struggle.

Give a little,
Make it simple
Making life manageable
For those still in the struggle

24/04/2000

Then smile is a poem about someone finding light in darkness!

THEN SMILE

If only someone could see me,
On the inside of me,
A side of me that only I can see.

Some days it's raining,
From morning till evening.

Then you would smile,
Smile for me.

And then it's a day of overcast,
Clouds hanging low,
When to it, there is no flow.

So what, with a mouth full of white teeth,
You have a good reason to smile,
So smile for me.

09/11/1999

A poem dedicated to my nieces and nephews

M.I.A, M.I.A

My niece and nephews,
Sorry I am yet to know you,
But a rebel had to do what a rebel had to do.

Prisoners of war,
From the shop corner to the University,
Living on the edge fighting the unseen enemy,
A destination to the graveyard or the penitentiary.

Off the battlefields,
Lasting wounds, wounds yet to heal.
It's like the 7 seals
The secrets seals
On the battlefields.

M.I.A, M.I.A.

In my head, post-traumatic stress dis-order
It happen, no it didn't,
But he didn't come back.

M.I.A, M.I.A

To my niece and my nephew,
Sorry I wasn't there to know you.
Still a rebel had to do what a rebel had to do.

PTSD M.I.A, M.I.A

26/04/2000

This poem reflects a time when hope was all I had and when time became a reflection point

IT'S TIME-LESS

This journey,
This journey.

A period, a dash,
How far have we come?
From then, to now
Can you see, see the sun?

A day, a month, years have passed,
Still, it seems, time stood still.

This journey,
It's timeless.

No one knows when the time will come,
That day may just be around the corner,
Who could tell?
No one knows.

Now, it makes me weary,
It's all in my mind, my soul and my body.
No one knows when the time is near.

How long I have been travelling?
I met a bear and a turtle,
They speak not a word, they just stared ahead,
Then I saw a rat and a Viper,
Squaring off against each other.

This journey this journey,
How far have I come?
A period, a dash,
No, I will never turn back.

This journey, it's timeless.

24/04/1999

When the judge gave me my sentence, I felt nothing, no concern, no remorse and yes, I felt no pain. However as time passes by, and the reality of prison started to sink in the reality and meaning true meaning of the word pain began to take hold I could only shook my head for the pain that I have hidden from for so many years was now at my doors.

PAIN

I feel your pain, I feel your pain,
Where would we be without pain?
I feel your pain, I feel your pain.

Through the many toils of life,
The difficulties and hardship,
Adversity and struggles,
They say we are made strong.

Like the sharpen blade of a knife,
And so we travel through life,
Reaching for new heights.

And so the Wiseman, ask again,
Where would we be without pain?
Then, the answer came

For some it's about survival,
The only way they know,
By the sweat of your brows.

Pain brought us here the Wiseman said,
A reward so beautiful, one worthy of pain,

He said, without the first pain, the pain of childbirth,
I would not have been here.

One out of a million sperm cells,
Traveling through space and time,
Up through the virginal passageway,
And then with nine months away,
It was pain that brought us here, the Wiseman says.

The pain and struggles of life made us stronger,
Build our character,
Consciousness, empathy and consideration for another.
The pain of my brother, the pain of my sister,

Pain that heals, pain purifies.
Yes, now I feel your pain.

06/08/2008

I broke my right forearm in June of 2002, this accident sent me to the hospital for a long time because the injury got infected. During my stay in the hospital it was as if I had born again. From that situation I wrote this poem.

THE BOX

Once there was a mighty deity
Traveling across a country
When he came upon a great big box deep in a valley

At first he turned his face
The box was lodged between a rock and a hard place
Then as he begun to pick up his pace
He remembered a story about a dark race

A race of people
Though by nature was created humble
Got captured wrapped in a bungle
Stuffed in a box and cast in a dark jungle

Remembering the story he was trouble
Turning away, he was unable
Indeed he had a title
The holy Quran and a Bible

Having the necessary tools at his disposal
Prying the box loose for disposal
For him would be easy, he had the necessary credential

Working all day and all night
Checking every sign in sight
Removing that big box would take all his might

A mighty deity, not one to run from a fight
From the sun he receive his life
Still it was not until the third night
When he first saw the light
In the middle of the wilderness the box stood upright

A bit shock, aloud he wondered
Oh great box, what secret though gather?
Then to his surprise, from the box came an answer

400 years of physical and mental torture
I carry the marks of those who were murdered
The deity was startled, what is this he wondered

We came from the lands of the east
We were attacked by a great big beast
Who has taken our throne and now sits in our royal seat

The language that he heard a language the ancients speak
Now a face from the box, a face he dare to meet
A people he might have to teach

Still no open to the box was there for him to see
This was a people locked in a box and cast beyond the sea
How could I, to a people longing to be free
Walk away, when it could easily have been me

A mighty deity
In his hands he had the key

Up to the box he went
The shirt of his garment he rent
For he was a saviour sent

Not a word of anger did he vent
For to every people a messenger was sent
Lifting up the box, exerting a fraction of his strength

Then for three and a half years
Upon his shoulder, a heavy burden he bears

Without a glimmer of fear
The burden of the oppressed, he carried with love and care
From his heart, to each of them his wisdom he share

Through the hills and the valley
That great big box he carry

Then with a thunderous sound
That great big box hit the ground
For his burden he laid down
At an instant, to the box an opening was found
Then out came an ancient people, who
once sat upon the throne

So it was, from that great big box a people came
A people now called by his name
Cry no more, cry no more for I share your pain

For you I have set a path
With the love from my heart
Three and a half years, you I have taught

Now my work in done
Out of captivity the kingdom of God has come

26/09/2002

This poem is one designed for you to see the glass as half full instead of half empty, enjoying life no matter the hand you have to deal with.

LIVE LIFE TO THE FULLEST

It might be a little rough around the edge, no reason not to live
Live life to the fullest

No matter what the situation
It could be worse, consider those who has no feet nor hand
Consider those living in faraway land
Where famine, drought and war are
killing people in the thousand
Where the weak are preyed upon

Even if you think it's a test
Just do your best
Life was never meant to be a bed of rose, no need to fret

Until that day when we are laid to rest
Let's just live our lives to the fullest
This is the life we have
Give thanks, it's more than most that pass away have

Smile a little
Laugh a little
No need to be brittle
Keep your eyes open

It's not that hard to understand
Sometimes you might be right, sometimes you may be wrong
Still this world is in your hand

Nothing else in creation
Could rule the earth and exploit the land
To you and me, the Gods have given dominion

So just live, live life to the fullest

There is a million reasons to do so
It's doesn't matter where we go

This is life, live it in your own little way
As we go from day to day
Just live life in your own little way

Just live, live life to the fullest

14/11/2001

The coverage by the media of hurricane Katrina, motivated the writing of this poem. The press, both print and electronic seems to have taken a tact to paint victims of the disaster as criminal when in fact, people were dying, and the government seems incapable of doing anything to help and save lives

ONE EYED BANDIT

One eyed bandit, one eyed bandit

Have him in the living room
The kitchen, the bedroom even in the bathroom

Never goes to sleep
Using words and pictures, it's the mind
of the children they seeks

Always telling tales, lies and spreading rumours
Make believe for you and me
A mystery
Trick-no-logy
How to live, where to go, who to see

One eyed bandit
One eyed bandit

Floor sized, table size even hanging from a wall
In churches, schools even in the shopping mall
Programs to keep you focus, answering every call

Words and sounds you rarely ever miss
Sell this
Buy this
Like this
Hate this

So say the one-eyed bandit
And there we sit
Digesting all of it

It tells us how to think, how to talk
How to laugh
Even how your day should start
Clothes to wear, food to eat, how great
you are before tearing you apart

Walking in a room, it sure to draw your attention
No matter your intention
Or the occasion

One eyed bandit always have you to change your plan
Sending you in a different direction

It could be movie
A commercial or a feel-good story
All designed to mislead you not to be
trusting of your own family
One eyed bandit
One eyed bandit

I often wonder how you are able
To control and fool so many people
Making even the strong to crumble

Your techniques so subtle
Tricks and games that goes un-notice-able
Damn! We the people
Are so naïve and gullible

In the living room
The kitchen the bedroom
Even in the bathroom
Programs that are sending our children to their doom

One eyed bandit
One eyed bandit
How do u do it?

25/09/2005

I had to get up and say no more, I had to change my habits, sometimes we have to changes our habits.

OLD HABITS, OLD HABIT

Old habits, old habits
Can't have this
Can't have this

Preparation
Application
Make a resolution

Try to find the will to move forward
To make a change and get something new done
We have nowhere to hide, nowhere to run

They tell me God will never change the condition of a person
Until that person begins to change the conditions of himself

Can't lock your secrets on a shelf
Or sit in a closet by yourself
There is always someone who could help

There will be doubters
Critics and even haters
Just don't be like the procrastinators

Always peeping through windows
looking around corners

Old habits, old habits
Can't have this
Won't have this

Hiding behind walls and shutters
Fighting for self and character
Let the staring eyes wonder
As you grow and get stronger

The harder it gets, the harder you push
Keep on pushing and pushing

The harder it gets, the harder you push
Keep on pushing and pushing

With your life you took that risk
Down death's lane you took that trip
Could it be, it was all a trick?

Bit by bit
Chip by chip
A new day, a new year you will change this
Old habit, old habit
Can't have this

With a little preparation
A little application
Make a resolution

Old habits, old habits
Can't have this
Won't have this

22/02/2003

YOU THINK

You think I have become weakened by your words?
I have become smaller by your criticism?
You think my once fire has been extinguished?

Well hear me loudly,

Your words demanded my strength!
I have become greater in my resurgence
from your enforced pit of despair!
The darkness by which you thought to oppress me
Like the caged hen, just to produce and die!

That darkness served just as incubation
time for my life anew to be born,
My flowering to reveal,
The brighter bud of vibrant red,
Red as the forged iron that is my present strength.

You thought wrong, yes!

By Joanne K Hallan

10/10/18

BELOW FOR OTHER PUBLISHED WORK BY DESMOND S. SKYERS, THE AUTHOR

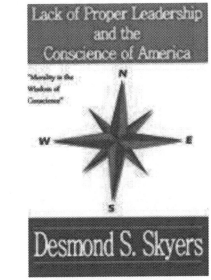

LACK OF PROPER LEADERSHIP AND
THE CONSCIENCE OF AMERICA

THE JAMAICAN GANGS OF NEW YORK

Printed in the United States
By Bookmasters